The Glass House

Also by Daniel Mark Epstein

POETRY
No Vacancies in Hell
The Follies
Young Men's Gold
The Book of Fortune
Spirits
The Boy in the Well
The Traveler's Calendar

PROSE
Star of Wonder
Love's Compass
Sister Aimee: The Life of Aimee Semple McPherson
Nat King Cole
*What Lips My Lips Have Kissed: The Loves and Love Poems of
    Edna St. Vincent Millay*
Lincoln and Whitman: Parallel Lives in Civil War Washington
The Lincolns: Portrait of a Marriage
Lincoln's Men: The President and His Private Secretaries

PLAYS
Jenny and the Phoenix
The Midnight Visitor
The Leading Lady
Jefferson and Poe

TRANSLATION
The Trinummus of Plautus (from the Latin)
The Bacchae of Euripides (from the Greek)

The Glass House

NEW POEMS

Daniel Mark Epstein

LOUISIANA STATE UNIVERSITY PRESS

BATON ROUGE

Published by Louisiana State University Press
Copyright © 2009 by Daniel Mark Epstein
All rights reserved
Manufactured in the United States of America
First printing

Designer: Laura Roubique Gleason
Typeface: Arno Pro
Printer and binder: Thomson-Shore, Inc.

Library of Congress Cataloging-in-Publication Data
Epstein, Daniel Mark.
  The glass house : new poems / Daniel Mark Epstein.
    p. cm.
  ISBN 978-0-8071-3410-8 (cloth : alk. paper) — ISBN 978-0-8071-3411-5 (pbk. : alk.
paper)
  I. Title.
PS3555.P65G57 2009
811'.54—dc22

2008032669

The paper in this book meets the guidelines for permanence and durability of the
Committee on Production Guidelines for Book Longevity of the Council on Library
Resources. ∞

Grateful acknowledgment is made to the editors of the following magazines in
which these poems first appeared: *Agenda* (England), *Atlanta Review, Chelsea,
Dalhousie Review* (Canada), *Georgia Review, Kenyon Review, Literary Review, Little
Patuxent Review, Michigan Quarterly Review, National Review, New Criterion, New
York Sun, OnEarth, Open City, Per Contra, Poetry Magazine, Raritan, Sewanee Review,
Shenandoah, Smartish Pace, Southern Review,* and *Southwest Review.*

For Anne Tyler

Contents

1

Vision at Dawn

1

I was wide awake before the wind.
Bands of coral clouds upon the azure
Horizon, bright above the lagging sun,
Closed like a louvered blind
Before I found words for the color.
Was there no painter at the easel?
Was I the only one at his window,
On a sleepy street or field of frost,
Who glimpsed the passing miracle?
A lonely thought—chilling as a ghost.
I bundled a blanket over my shoulders.

Maybe one of my children, or neighbors
Would telephone to tell me they had seen
What I remember now uncertainly:
The sky was layered gold, then it was grey
(Or sliced with coral-red, incarnadine?)
Before the sun came crashing into day
To waken the world to its common vision.

2

What Death reveals to you He keeps from me;
This is not cruelty but natural law.
The thought that no one else saw what I saw
Is brother to the darker notion
That what everyone sees I could not see,
And this is a heartache as one grows old.
There is the wide sky, the hill, the ocean,
The maple tree once draped in shingled gold
That now bares its skeleton
To host the crow when the songbird is gone.

Refrain

These days when you hear the sea scaling the sand
        a hundred miles away,
These summer days when the dawn curls open
        like the seashell's ear,
And the Capitol is empty as a congressman's skull
        during adjournment,
School is out, the blackboard black, chairs upturned
        on desks, legs in the air,
These days when the black-eyed Susans run
        riot in the flowerbed,
These summer days when the wind is calm
        as a tamed lion
Except for the fitful squalls that turn the leaves
        silver and ruffle the lawn,
Out comes the sun and dries up all the rain.
        It is an old refrain.

These days no one works but those who can't help it,
        like the very rich and poor;
The priest, the postman, the undertaker, the poet,
        and the bees work overtime
These summer days, in the panicles of fringed petals
        of the crape myrtle,
For it is bees' business to make the trees immortal,
        that stand so still.
These summer days that hold the noon sun
        in golden suspension,
Long days fearless of night, the moon's phases,
        and mindless of October,
These summer days the children's voices echo
        in the boxwood maze,
Until their heads reach above hedgetops—they outgrow
        one labyrinth and enter another—

These summer days, as teenage boys doing ninety
          in their top-down cars,
And tattooed girls chain-smoking cigarettes
          think they will never die
While their grandmothers turning ninety in shut rooms
          pray the angel will pass by,
Leaving a white feather on the windowsill.
          These summer days
When each of us is alive and immortal
          in this blazing moment,
Praising the sun, the sea, the bees, the old and young,
          the past and lucky present;
These summer days that put off night for hours
          in their desire to please,
These days you think you could live forever
          and you just might.

The Pure Gift

In Memoriam LME

On the hottest day that summer, a rainbow
Arced over the clock-tower of the brick pile
We call The Rotunda, a dying shopping mall
With a wilting grocery, a druggist, a flower stall,
A dozen half-lit vacant retail stores
And a crafts gallery. I had just bought
A jewel box, the lid a parquet braid
Of spruce and rosewood artfully inlaid,
With a comb of music teeth to play a tune
For one who might never open it to listen.

There is a clear-cut purity in the gift
Purchased with love that may not be returned.
I walked out into twilight holding the treasure
The clerk had gift-wrapped in white paper
And bound with ribbons, silver and turquoise
All cunningly curled. Then I looked up
And saw the rainbow against the violet sky
Late in the rainless day, bold and unbidden.
No gold anchors the generous bridge of heaven.

The Final Exam

They had turned in their bluebooks and gone,
All but one, whose eyes welled with tears.
The teacher would not rush her. He was kind.
It was the end of the term, the end of autumn;
Yellow leaves tumbled, spun across the lawn.
Time to go home and leave the books behind,
The mysteries of life and human frailty,
Free will and determinism, "Buridan's ass,"
Which posed the essay question that came last.
The hungry beast was led between haystacks
Identically delectable, each a perfect feast.
But then a cruel fabulist had trapped
Him midway between temptations, so that
While he drooled he could not budge,
Moment to moment, for he could not choose.
The sun had risen and set upon the wretch,
His wasted flanks and then a pile of bones,
Since the Middle Ages. Maybe the bright girl
Was grieving over this. *It is not a fair match:*
Pitting freedom and fate against each other.
And let none of us presume to fathom
What made the pupil and her young teacher
(Who wanted years enough to make him wise)
Forget the pen, the beast, the philosophy class.
At last he drew near and touched her shoulder,
And they led each other gently into the world.

Fleur-de-Lys

When sepals and petals look the same,
As in the tiger lily, we call them
Tepals, these bright blades of perianth,
Sheathing the tulip and hyacinth,
The blossoms that do not bother to put on
Green calyx beneath the corolla gown.

If all this is Greek to us, then
So it is. Most of the savory words
That make a flower: anther, stamen,
(Not pistil, which some Roman
Named because its style reminded him
Of his pestle, and his swords),

Were spoken by Aristotle and Phidias,
Long ago, by hero, virgin, and wench.
Much later came the tepal, coined in Paris.
Once the ancient gardeners were done
Spinning flowers from words, no one
Dabbled in such magic but the French.

The View

The scarlet torches of crape myrtle
Crowd my window, kindled by the sun.
Their thick foliage blocks my view

Of all but the treetops and the sky.
I enjoy the flower-clusters, and butterflies
That visit here, green midges, and bees

That traffic in nectar and yellow pollen.
I might still learn economy or lore
From their abrupt, impulsive intimacy.

But I am jealous of the light that's lost
To these gorgeous interlopers that began
Five years ago and twenty feet below

As blooming shrubs against the wall.
I remember the castle in a fairy tale,
Overgrown with brambles, trees, and vines,

Fallen under a curse, or witch's spell,
Lost to the world for years, impenetrable—
A house where only sleep was possible.

I cannot see the garden for the flowers.
Time to throw open the sash. Be merciless!
Out with the shears, off with their pretty heads.

The Comb-Bearers

Some windless nights on Narragansett Bay,
The inlet looks like a field of green fireflies
As multitudes of the luminous jellyfish
Called "comb-bearers" float to the surface
For no evident purpose
But to amaze the fishermen and scientists

Who know them only slightly, each one no more
Than a pear-shaped living sack of liquid
With skin thinner than tissue paper, a sheer piece
Of moonlight on the sea, so fragile
The least ripple may tear it
To bits. Calm evenings, the amber-green species

May spread out over a thousand yards square,
An island made of bright individuals
Who usually live in the depths, a zone where
Wave movement ceases. Only on nights
Like these do the comb-bearers
Rise, when the bay lies still as a sheet of slate.

Loveliest of sea beings, the color
Of spring arbutus or pink anemone,
As some pass beneath the surface of the water
The effect is of rainbow glory
More seductive than moonlight
To the naturalist who might try to scoop one up

Ever-so-gently in his fine net and
Hold it awhile in a clear beaker of brine—
Perhaps the giant of the race, "Venus's girdle,"
Come from the Mediterranean—

An iridescent ribbon
Which vanishes en route to the laboratory.

The advantage of their luminescence
Is unknown, being of doubtful value in
Luring prey. As for mating: it is difficult
To imagine that these delicate,
Melting creatures could sustain
The violence of lovemaking. Yet they make light.

Dead Reckoning

Halfway between the familiar harbor
And our destination, soon it seemed
Partway between nowhere and nowhere;
The stars we counted on to plot our course
Fled before a mass of ghostly clouds.
And there was nothing more to guide us
But the ship's log and compass,
A scribbled record of our starting out
And the wobbling arrow of direction,
Vague tokens of the past and present,
And the sensation of speed and distance
In the puffed sail, the rope in our wake.
As for the future: the vision of a coast
Unknown and indescribable seemed
The more precious the longer we were lost.
Day dawned upon fog as dense as night.
And some, after many days like this
Turn upon each other in blind rage,
Dive headlong from the foretop,
Or drown in grog, forgetting
Why we ever left home, signed on
For such a voyage, to a land unknown
When nothing had been promised beyond hope.

Hope

In winter the crescent moon vanishes
So quickly in the blue, down the horizon,
Between the starry darkness and morning,

Like the hull of a ship without rigging
That I was meaning to load with wishes,
O not for me, my dear, wishes for you,

And you and you, my friends, all of us,
Such cargo as could only ride upon
The silver shell of that hallowed galleon.

I daydreamed, got bewildered by my muse,
Sun on the lace of frost, and fading Venus.
I looked up, and the reckless moon had gone.

2

The Frame

In the heat of writing about you
In a blank book, my special one,
I skipped a page, wastefully.
When I thought I was through,
Turning back to where I'd begun,

I noticed this white space,
Speechless, peaceful, pure as only
Silence ever could be
Or will be, ever again:
The hush after hard rain,

Of a rosebud blowing open;
The lull that comes darkly
After someone has misspoken
And nobody knows what to say;
The quiet that fills a room

When death visits the house,
As the spirit hovers in place
And grievers have not yet
Seen it rise above the bed
And turn the color of air.

In the rush to finish my verse
About you, I left a space—
An empty foursquare frame.
And there I saw your face,
More haunting than any poem.

The Neighbor's Garden

I am the luckiest man in the month of May
To look out my high window
On such a plot, and a gardener more lovely
Than the columbine, fox-glove and anemone
She tends with her cunning fingers. So rare!
She stands barefoot among bearded irises
Or kneels to weed as they bow to the glories
Of her bright skin, the roundness of a cheek
Her auburn hair pinned at the nape lays bare.

She rises—most graceful when she stands—
Arms loose at her sides, trowel in hand,
Head cocked, pensive, eager but patient,
Waiting for seeds to take root in the ground
Or buds to blossom.
                        Just so, at twilight,
Despite the untold blessings of my life,
I wait for the spring splendor to be ruined
By wind and rainstorm, hail and hurricane,
Leaving bleak relics, thistle, straw, and chaff.

I hear tomorrow is her wedding day.
A verdant faith glows in her mild eyes.
She clips some roses from a trellised bush,
Suddenly shades her vision with one hand,
And looks up at the window where I hide
In shadow. Laws of light and darkness say
She is the body visible, not I;
And yet she waves to me, the smiling bride.
Hello, my darling, good luck, and good-bye.

Alice

She had come to the place
Just shy of womanhood,
Seeing and being seen
Lovely of form and face,
That cannot come to good
Without some sheltering grace.

Men would stop and stare,
Then turn away, ashamed
Of what they dare not do
And where they might not go,
If madness could be blamed.
Free of pride and vanity

As if she'd been born blind
Or never held a mirror,
She passed in her summer dress,
So oblivious of her beauty
She might search for its likeness
Behind the looking glass and not before.

The Lady Slipper

Into a virgin wood west of Terra Alta
You took me one afternoon in May
To see the bed of lady slipper orchids.
Since girlhood you had kept them secret
So that one spring day you might
Go there as a woman with a man
And find the wild pink orchids blooming still.
You were seventeen; I was a few years older.

In a muslin blouse tied with red ribbons,
You led me by the hand, laughing,
Past cranberry bogs and deep into the pines.
And if I thought you were too young,
I had no heart or mind but to follow you
And see those flowers beloved of Venus,
So delicate and rare they scarce can bear
A man's gaze, let alone the human touch.

In the shade they glowed, the colony
Of flowers, each rising on its green fuse
Out of a crotch of deep-ridged oval leaves,
Each rose-pink blossom with its sac-like lips
Around the pouch netted with purple veins.
And when I turned around we both were naked.
We made our bed in the hurrying light
On a knoll of moss above the bed of orchids.

Cleome

Sunbeams are sweeping the mist away
And soon will unwind the furled rose mallow,
Those white whirligigs with scarlet hearts
That worship morning.
                You've been gone
For days now, and the garden you made
Has never been such a feast for the eyes,
Bees and rabbits, birds and butterflies;
Red-lipped poppies, purple mourning brides,
Mauveine echinacea gemmed with seeds
Goldfinches come to plunder. And Cleome,
The flower whose name you love to say,
Cleome, with feathery petals pink and white,
Bursts from long-stalked pods like fireworks
Of little orchids in July.
                Tall hollyhocks,
Argus-eyed, stand guard all day and night.
Cleome . . . the strange melodious sound
Meant nothing to me, and cannot be found
In ancient folklore where such names are born,
But must have murmured up out of the ground
Somewhere near the Tropic of Capricorn.

It is my humble duty to report
In ragged rhythm and haphazard rhyme,
A vision that the muses brought to me
Concerning this nymph, the dryad Cleome,
Nearly immortal. In her beauty's prime
She'd outlived a phoenix or two, seven
Stags, five ravens and a flock of crows,
And then nine generations of strong men.
She was kind when she was not cruel to us.

Cleome had the power of divination
And a green thumb. She made gardens
Thrive in city plots, so colorful
And haunting, each seemed a tapestry
Fresh from a Flemish loom of the Gobelins.
At long last she fell in love with a man
Unlike any born in all the centuries,
Who had a power she had never known,
To make her love him in the mortal way.
And being at the short end of her span
(Though no one knew but she, for Time
Never laid a hand on her hair or skin)
She wept to foresee she might outlive him.

Outside their window while her lover slept,
Dreaming an old man's good dream of youth,
She lay down in the garden she had kept
In the light of her lingering beauty.
She shrank under the stars to a glowing root,
Whence at daybreak bloomed the white Cleome.

Ronsard's Dream

O wouldn't I love to be the golden rain
Drenching the bare thighs of Madeleine
As she sleeps, or tries to, in the downpour;

Wouldn't I love to be the great white bull
Who takes her as she goes over the hill
In April, a flower amazing the other flowers;

Wouldn't I love to slake the thirst of lovers,
Play Narcissus, making the nymph my pool,
And plunge into her all night long;

If only then that night could be eternal,
And dawn kindly refuse to rekindle
A new day—and mine be the last song.

Out of the Astral Air

for Jennifer

Out of the astral air, love visits us,
Seeding the heart, spreading its blessings
Abroad in life and song, like the lotus
Pollen swans transport upon their wings
In coupling, that drifts on to conceive
Pink water lilies on the valley pool.
Bold and curious the woman was
Who could have loved a god instead of me—
A being free of time and pain and grief.
I think it is a singular miracle
She was not afraid, or blinded by glory,
But chose a weary man whose brow
Is marked by death and sorrow,
Finding him somehow more beautiful.

Obsession

I study the hours on an heirloom watch,
Precious hours marked with diamonds
That scatter the sunlight over the room.
Since you left, I am obsessed with time,
Unsure if it is my enemy or my friend,
Knowing that all suffering ends in time.
I wonder if minutes might be redeemed
To some purpose, palliative and kind,
By watching them pass under the second hand,
Or spill in a silver stream through the hourglass,
The wavering thread of sand creating
A pyramid of minutes from its domed tower,
Where a phantom finger gently pushes down
On the white drift until the hour is over.

The hands of the pendulum clock atone
At noon, point to the zenith where the sun
Looks down upon our garden. Alone here
I ransom an hour of daylight,
Hovering over the gnomon of the sundial.
I'm furious at time, which has no end
And no beginning, no heart or balm to heal,
Blind with grief, sun-stricken and unable
To tell by sight an enemy from a friend.

In Late November

Of the butterfly bush, whose purple flowers
The monarch and the swallowtail
Sipped in August, near my windowpane
(Such a wealth of wings and flower clusters
I could hardly see the grass, the trees)
Only stalks and branches remain,
And panicles tipped with russet berries.

Now I see everything so vividly:
The young woman on her hands and knees,
Planting the meek shrubs three years ago—
Three short years and thirteen feet below—
Told me the light was perfect here and so
The plants would thrive, just wait and see
How gracefully the flowers would bear wings.

I would see her when she was not there,
Then go blind, standing right beside her.
How could I begin to explain such things?
Soon enough the blossoms reached my sill,
A floor above her terrace flat. Too late
For her to see the wonder she had wrought
Or for me to tell her. She'd moved out.

I never dreamed these branches in full bloom
Would all but block the summer view below:
Garden, gardener and terrace door,
Casting a dappled shadow across my room.
I never knew that when November came
I would miss the butterflies so much
And see the world more clearly than before.

The Everlastings

In a stream of mid-morning winter light
The lavender spray your silver ribbon bound
Hangs upside down from a pin, as bright
As any blue we ever saw in the garden.
With such great gifts, I suppose you might
Have done the same with your strawflower,
Or "cupid's dart," any everlasting,
The fire amaranth with its scarlet leaves,
The globe amaranth, or "love-lies-bleeding,"
With its drooping tassels of red flower spikes
That feel like chenille to the touch.
Such names! Who but a heartbroken
Gardener would make up such a name?

Some ancient Greek named a pure fiction
Amaranth, the myth of an unfading flower,
Never supposing you might make it real
By picking these blooms just as they open
From the bud, before light can turn them brown,
Stripping the leaves, hanging them upside down
In bundles like this one hugged by a band
Until the heat of hearth and home has drawn
The last pearl of moisture from the stems.
For love you left me the lavender, fragrant,
And kept for your own the crown of amaranth
By which, in keeping with an ancient spell,
You've turned immortal and invisible.

Edna St. Vincent Millay

(1892–1950)

Unquiet spirit, by what right
Do I come to disturb your dust
In this omniscient October light
A half century almost from the day
You tumbled down your library stairs
Into eternal night? By what right
Do I invade the dignity of your house,
Ransack the closets, shelves and drawers,
Measuring your dresses and jewelry,
Picturing you alive, challenging me?

I breathe deep, hoping a sweet scent
Of you, long breathless, might arise,
Some stray atom of your spirit meant
For mine alone. We are not so different
Maybe—man, woman, alive or dead,
Souls confronting the inarticulate.

I come to write your life, a ghoulish trade—
Like others of my time and not like you
Who made a fortune making Fortune rhyme.
To make my living I must turn to prose.
This is what has brought me to your house,
Gardens, letters, grave and diary.
And if you didn't want biography,
Why do you preserve all of this stuff,
Your books, shoes and teacups, lingerie,
A hat made from a peacock, golden coat
Cut from a lion or an ocelot?

The fiery swirl of hair clipped from your head
In childhood to make tresses for a doll;
The doll itself! Sits staring, cracked and bald
Above the bureau where the hair is kept,
The relic of a goddess, wrapped
In tissue, the red hair that drove men mad,
Made them write love letters by the yard,
Pleading, jealous, tormented by need,
Ready to die or kill for love of you.
You kept them all. Had you no regard
For the dignity of the dead, no modesty?
Did you mean to burn them before you died?
I want to think you left the hoard for me,
Calling me to bring you back to life,
Dangerous, voluptuous, green-eyed:
Better a poet, moonlighting biography
Than a shrunken scholar, deaf to prosody.

I want to believe it. But who am I
To climb this wooded hill
Along an overgrown, untrodden trail,
To touch the gravestone planted in
The earth that owns your ashes still,
Joined with your husband, your true love,
Here in this mountain laurel grove?

I bow my head, a living question mark.
The world was yours: beauty, love and fame,
The gift of speech, moments of ecstasy,
Money and men, houses, horses, land.
Why, Edna, were you never satisfied?
Can I write what I cannot understand?

I have yet to check the one-room shack
Where you wrote a libretto and a book
Of verse before your beauty and your art
Gave in to gin, morphine, and despair.
Heart pounding, I loose the rusted lock.
Nothing here but a table and chair,
An iron wood-stove and a wind-up clock
On the windowsill, faded, vague with dust,
Whose hands were tied one autumn afternoon
Or early morning fifty years ago.
At last! Is this the sign I begged for, some
Sympathetic magic, a poet's trick?
Across the timeless space I hear the rhythm;
The clock, true as a heart, begins to tick.

Now you tell me what you learned too late:
True joy, like genius, is a grace
To nurture, bring to blossom and bear fruit
In its own season. Thundering ecstasy
Always may be bought for the right price
Of wine or the poppy, sex or poetry.
Death to the soul that cannot see
The difference. Lightning blasts the house
Built to be the home for happiness.

The Jealous Man

Soul-sick, he cannot sleep. Outside,
Hydra, the old dragon of chaos,
Coils across the moonless winter sky.
On its back the Crow and Goblet ride,
Constellations the magi identified
Long ago, sailor, lover, insomniac,
All who have lost, yearned to recover
Their paths. Soon real crows will come
Vexing the dawn with cries, blotting the oak.

Who but a stargazer would have known
The crow was silver once, Apollo's pet
Raven? Then the god in fury cursed
The gossip bird for telling him his mistress
Coronis played him false with a mere man;
Cursed the bird black and shot the fickle woman
With an arrow aimed so neatly through the heart
Even his art couldn't heal her. Better, he thought,
It would have been if he had never known.

The night is long, the tale is not yet done.
Hating himself then, hating the strung bow,
The arrow and the angry hand that notched it,
Although he was a god what could he do?
Drink from the goblet on the dragon's back
For courage, and carve into the steaming womb
Of his dead love, bringing to light his baby boy
Who one day with serpent-coiled staff,
Would heal the lame and sick, and baffle death.

Curses

after Mellin de Saint-Gelais

May the Lord make you a pauper,
A homeless old man without
An ear of corn in the barn, not
A bottle of wine in the cellar.

Until then, I pray by right and reason,
Home shall bring you no pleasure,
So for comfort you may prefer
To commit crimes, and rest in prison.

Or may you be forced into exile,
Anonymous among rude strangers,
To beg for rancid leftovers,
Without words for hunger. Meanwhile,

Stand outside her door in your cashmere
Coat in a storm, under the rainspout
All night long, cry out
For her to open, but she will not hear.

The Widower's Journey

In and out of the mountain,
I ride on the railroad train.
As the coach lights go down,
My inward eye recovers.
Day funnels into darkness,
Then tunnels to light again.
Across from me two lovers
Are using the gloom to kiss.

I am untroubled by this.
But something is troubling her,
I think. He is uncertain.
The future is dark to us . . .
A mercy! I long to say
(Too shy for the intrusion)
We see sorrows one by one.
But this is not my play.

He answers whatever she asks,
His smile overturns her frown.
Tragic and comic masks
Overlook the stage curtain:
One fears it will come down,
One laughs that it must open.
The train rolls under the mountain
Where all of us travel alone.

Old Wives' Tale

I have picked a spray of mallow
By moonlight, for its powers;
So ghostly white, the blossoms,
From petals to pistil and stamens,
All of a uniform pallor—no
One ever saw such flowers.

And if you really have left me
After all we have known,
Vows broken and mended dearly,
Seeds gathered, saved and sown;
If you're gone, and as legend has it,
Nature, reason, or rhyme

Commands your body and spirit:
Return to the scene of the crime,
You will see a bouquet of mallow
Dawn in the blue porcelain
Vase here in my window,
Remember our love, and come home.

3

The Glass House

Where should I cast my sorrow
If not here beneath these maple trees
At the lake's edge, with a wishing stone
The cold weight of my heart,
Wishing what has come might be undone?
In the glass house of dawn

Where shall I cast my cracked pebble:
At my own image rising from dry grass,
Purple loosestrife, asters and goldenrod,
Or beyond, where black water limns a cloud
Rainbow-winged, like a truant angel,
Or drowns the sparrow on the bough?

His song goes rippling on in trills
No lake can trace or echo.
Like the morning mirrored in the gloom,
The fallen world defies the world of grace.
Where shall I cast my stone
If not at the dark portrait of my face?

The Sleeping Messenger

As if a god had crushed the firmament
Into a glittering ball,
Then spread the chart as a portent,
Heaven is in chaos. Let the prophet
Go blind, he will shed no light on it.

The old messenger has his directions
To warn us of gales at sea,
Rape in the hay, the freak accidents
Of birth and death, faithfully
To bear the valid letter of reprieve.

But time has overtaken him in his course.
His eyelids are heavy with the grief
Of so much failure, so many miles.
Hours away the day dawns on catastrophes
While he sleeps under a crinkled map of stars.

The Good Doctors

July: blue sage and lavender heal the earth.
And I have written not a rag of verse
Since April Fool's Day, when the doctors
Said because of an accident of birth,
A stray gene, some rare glitch in the brain
My boy might never reason like a man.
For me it was as if he had died,
Someone I had loved but never known.

Under the harsh lights, none of us could hide.
Because he could not talk or ring a bell
Like other toddlers, put the peg in a hole,
They had removed his body from its soul,
Probing for the mind that binds us all.
And it seemed to me unspeakably cruel
This child, with a great heart and a smile
Everyone who sees must repay in kind,
Should lack sufficient wit to tell—
In this world of falsehood and delusion—
Good from evil, wise from senseless men.
It seemed unthinkably cruel,
And I lost the cadence of a season
That April day in my grief, a broken fool.

Psalm of Pernett du Gillet

The night was so dark it had hidden heaven
And earth from me. To my despair,
At noon I could not see a human face,
Though I heard voices. So when dawn
Came rushing in, as if from nowhere,
With its thousand colors, and suddenly
I was surrounded by light, better late
Than never I joined in praising the glory
That led a new day through the broken gate.

An Icon Drawn in Wax on Cloth

after Manuel Philes, ca. 1275–1345

Now by what art or magic
Were you captured here,
Madonna, in this fabric;
How come the wax running from fire
Did not burn through the cloth?
Lord, Who once appeared
As a burning bush, thriving on
What could not be consumed,
I see You, resolved in truth,
Arise from an artist's fire.
Maybe You poured a potion
From heaven on the torch
He held who made this drawing,
So even strangers to church
Beholding the virgin's face,
Cannot but admit the grace
That dims the flames of suffering.

The Clockmaker

Time should be heard as well as seen,
Says the clockmaker, carving a cuckoo bird.
My wife gives the sick child his medicine.
Who said children should be seen, not heard?

I work all night until my sight is blurred,
At this abandoned craft that now is mine
For all the comfort folly can afford.
Time should be heard as well as seen.

I can't imagine what life might have been
Without the babies crying, had I preferred
The cloister or the study at nineteen,
Thinks the clockmaker carving a cuckoo bird

In hours stolen from sleep, pleasure deferred
For the sake of this obsession, a daft machine
That never can refund the cost incurred.
My wife gives the sick child his medicine

Praying he'll sleep soundly and be fine
Tonight or tomorrow night, someday. The third
Time he cried out wrecked my whole design.
Who said children should be seen, not heard?

I dreamed he lay so peaceful that the Lord
Himself believed the stillness was divine
And would not wake him, although my absurd
Clocks froze and went silent for a sign:
      Time should be heard.

The Clock at Wells Cathedral

So time might fairly be heard or seen
By all—the deaf, the blind, the simpleton—
Artisans once made clocks without hands.
Then the clock-jacks, painted manikins,
Came to strike these bells of copper and tin
Within the transept. *God cannot replace*
The quarter-hour lost, and God is good,
Bells remind the blind. The rest behold
Two mounted knights ride out and then
Tilt their tiny lances at each other.
Six hundred years in wartime and in peace,
Father and son, grandchild and grandmother
Have brought their kin (also the child within),
To watch one knock the other off his horse
At the stroke of the hour, the winner
And loser always the same, never the worse.

Omega

All day long my watch has been stopping
On me, every few hours, a good Omega
Automatic chronometer, certified,
Gold face and bezel, circa 1970,
Self-winding. My father left it to me
When he died, and never has the watch
Given me a minute's trouble. Maybe
Today I'm too still to keep it wound,
And it's much later than I thought;
Lost hours are shimmering into twilight.
I shake the timepiece, it awakens. I set
The hands that promise to keep moving,
Listen to be sure that we're still ticking.

He Makes His Mark

for Nathaniel

Back when only holy men could write,
The farmer or squire who signed himself
With the letter *X*, St. Andrew's cross,
Would bow and put his lips to it,
Reverently, in proof of his good faith.
Now: here's a boy knows only goodness
And honesty. Nature has denied
Him the gift of reason, yet he has made
His mark in the world. Guide
The pen as he scrawls, and bear witness.
His cross shall serve for a name and a kiss.

Lullaby

I sang to each of my children
When sleep came too slowly,
The words of a mystery
In a haunting minor tune:
Open the door softly,
I've something to tell you, dear.
Open it up no wider
Than the crack upon the floor.
Open the door softly,
I've something to tell you, dear.
I learned it from a street singer
Who promised me the rest
As soon as he could remember.
Now I hear he has died.
So I may never hear
Who knocked, who was inside,
What one had to say and why
The other would not open.
And not one of my children
Entranced by the lullaby
Ever turned in my arms
To ask what was unspoken
On the edge of oblivion.

4

Ponte Vedra

In the lightning-crazed sky above the sea
I cannot tell the angels from the clouds
Or any god's voice from thunder.
I have not had the heart for poetry
In half a year, being too much consumed
With birth, death, the hazard and the odds,
To see or hear the breath of my own wonder.

Not by calculus or strategy
Has anyone attained a paradise;
But standing on the stairway where surprise
Alights with its shower of gold, alive
In the hour extempore, wide-eyed, free
As a dolphin or seagull, one may be
Ready for the gods when they arrive.

Has that passage of exaltation scrolled
By me so quickly I did not catch the sense?
To be free, must we understand the world?
This point flows to a line, the line flows
Into a circle of words. Here I live in it
Day to day, the long rambling sentence
Doubling back on itself, ending in prose.

The Messenger

The movements of faith must constantly be made
by virtue of the absurd.
—SØREN KIERKEGAARD

Neither cherubim nor seraphim
Could bear the order. God Himself
Spoke those dire words to Abraham,
To take his only son into Moriah,
Three days from home. All that way
On foot and assback, he had to brood
Over the strange commands of Elohim.
They pressed on, father and son (the wood
To roast the lambkin stretched a saddlebag)
And two grown men for comfort or defense.
He was much too old, the boy too young
For such a journey, far from Beer-sheba;
The rocks hid brutal thieves and murderers
Moved by voices mortal and profane.

All this I saw as I hovered near the earth.
God told him to stab the child to death,
Then burn him on the altar, such and such
A mountain, He said, and His word was law.
Spying the crest God promised, he would not
Let his young friends travel the last mile
With him, but said: "Wait here with the ass
While I take the lad to worship yonder."
Loading the firewood upon his son,
He took torch in one hand, knife in the other;
And as they went the child thought it a game
They played. What a joy to be with father,
Alone at last! Though now his father seemed
A little lost and troubled. "I see the fire,"
The boy said. "Here is wood for sacrifice.
This must be the place. Where is the lamb?"
"God will provide," he replied. So He would.

The boy I think still thought this was a game
As father laid him down upon the sticks
And tied him there—except for the odd light
In those faithful eyes, and suddenly the knife.

All this I watched, and here I drew the line.
I am no special angel. Of the nine
Choirs I dwell farthest below the seat
Of the Most High and those Councillors
Who take their glory straight from God,
Or Powers who rule stars and wind and rain.
Little more than a muse am I, more kin
To Helicon's fair nine than the Lord's Thrones.
I whisper truth and guard the innocents.
Knowing the Lord had more then on His mind
Than one graybeard gone mad with piety,
I took it upon myself to countermand
Words spoken in a fit of jealousy
Of human love (He is a jealous God!).
Quick as a thought I flew to the man's side
And told him lay down his weapon, do
No harm to the child. "Put down the knife
Before he dies of fright or you of grief.
We see you would do anything God says
(Or think He said, for how can you be sure?)
And I am only an angel. Please believe
This word in your ear is equal to the Word
You heard or think you heard three days ago.
And look," I sang, "behind you toils a ram
Caught in a thicket, just as you are bound
In the wilderness of Moriah and your mind—
Between the past and present, death and life.
Give God the beast, old man; embrace your son."

The Suit

My grandfather, nineteen years of age,
Falls from the pages of the unabridged
Dictionary where I keep him pressed,
A sepia print of him in his second suit,
A double-breasted serge. The satin tie
Flows from a knot held by a silver pin.
His second suit. The first, he bought
With six years of savings, pennies earned
As cabin boy, deckhand, and seaman.
The night he put it on and went ashore
Some shipmate cracked wise about the cut
Of the cloth or the man who wore it, that
Somehow one was unsuited to the other,
The one being too fine, the other crude.
Whereupon my grandfather swung at him,
And one blow led to another until the men
Whirled into a blur of fisticuffs and blood,
Fought until their clothing was in tatters.

So now he appears in his second suit,
Bought off the rack in Hong Kong or London
Just after the Great War. He's tough
And handsome, bright-eyed, proud,
Daring the whole world to call his bluff,
Cocksure the clothes don't make the man.

Grandfather's Spectacles

He was not a brawler, or vain,
But came up in a time and class
Where a youth of exceptional beauty
Had to prove himself—man to man—
Time and again. Nearsightedness
Made him half-blind; so at fourteen
He went stumbling to the optician
Who ground him his first pair of spectacles.
Amazed by the view, he walked the streets
'Til dark, taken by leaves, pebbles, and stars,
Then the grin of a bully who demanded:
Drop the "frog-eyes" or he'd die laughing!
And in that fight, the first thing broken
Was the miraculous invention
Of wire and glass that let him see
The world and the cost of clear vision—
Ground to dust in the streets of the old city.

A Sense of Style

And in this frame great-grandmother looks lovely
      In her high-collared satin dress,
So many buttons! A button for every sin, as
      They used to say, and the stone
Cameo brooch that has come down to you, my dear.
      Long past her prime she maintained
A sense of style though somehow free of vanity,
      Unlike the pastor, her husband,
Who perhaps from too much Ecclesiastes,
      The *vanitas vanitatum,*
Was so obsessed with this he would not face a mirror
      Or the dark art of photography,
Said he would die first, which his wife took with a grain
      Of salt, or maybe not—we still
Wonder. But at last she hired Brady and assistant
      To come to the rectory on
Such and such a date when man and wife were to be
      At home, to take their portrait,
For there must be one for posterity, for all
      To read their lineaments.

And as it happened this was the very day my great-
      Grandfather chose to breathe his last,
A sad day for his widow certainly, and one
      Of confusion, not least because
The photographer arrived with his glass slides and
      Black box before the mortician,
Whereupon she sat the beloved in his chair, propped so,
      And stood beside him holding his hand,
(See, he looks a little drowsy and ill at ease),
      But she is smiling in that way they do
In the old photographs, having to hold the pose
      For what must have seemed an eternity.

A Friendly Visit

after the painting by William Merritt Chase

Two women on an absinthe-green banquette
Sit separated by the pink brocade
Length of a plumped pillow. Mid-morning.

A dark-haired beauty, young, arrayed
In lemon crepe de chine, black velvet
Neckband and waist ribbon, is listening

As an older woman, also splendid, dressed
In white satin and lace, speaks her mind.
The pointed arch of her hand pressed

On the coverlet, enforces her argument,
As does the furled flesh-colored parasol
She holds, making a point on the bare floor

That precisely divides the small apartment
With its wicker chairs and green wall,
Mirrors and pillows, oils and trumpery.

She has not removed her hat or the white veil
She hoped might make her less conspicuous
In this strange quarter where the vendors cry

Cherries and calf brains, rumpsteaks and filets,
And painters dabble in these ateliers.
There is nothing friendly about such visits.

The space between the women fits the man.
What does this mistress know about devotion?
What does the wife remember of his passion?

Tornado, 1911

from a diary

The inquest was reported in the press,
Words of experts, and eyewitnesses
Like me, one may read when I am dead.
She entered the schoolyard before class,
A frail blond girl, no better or worse

Than the rest of us, my mother said.
Kate shut the gate, put down her books,
Seemed about to join us on the swings,
Although she usually played alone.
Next thing we knew a gust of wind

That spun our hair and made a moan,
Lifted Kate Sullivan into the air—
Her arms extended as if to measure
An adventure of impossible breadth,
Her skirt blown out like a balloon.

The wind carried her higher and higher
As one who had been called to Heaven.
Surely the angel that drew her skyward
Would be kind enough to set her down
In this shaky world, or another, gently?

But it was just a funnel of wind alas
That turned her loose as quick and carelessly
As it had selected her from among us,
Dropped her from a height of thirty feet,
And the earth struck her without mercy.

The Vanishing Oriole

Orioles, common as robins when I was young,
Are going the way of the passenger pigeon
Whose mile-wide flocks two counties long
(According to John James Audubon)
Wheeled and coiled like serpents in the sky,
Shutting out the light of the noon sun.
Now nobody alive has ever seen one.

No hue in nature matches the oriole's breast,
That bright cadmium orange, except maybe
Marigolds when the sun is low. And I miss
The bird's staccato mezzo-soprano,
His pitch, so round and rich, his syncopation.
If he has a fault, it lies in the desultory
Treatment of his theme, a predilection

For chattering preludes and fiddlery before
The main melody—a fine construction.
Half-done, he'll take wing, leaving us to wonder
Who will sing the last notes, and when
And where, and who on earth will listen,
As if there were no end to the generations
Of passenger pigeons, orioles, songs and men.

After Whitman's "Lincoln Speech"

The cannons are all silent as the dead
Of that distant war, buried
Long ago, and their widows and children
Also entombed, burned, or lost at sea.
Now it all comes to this hazy distance,
Earth, fire, and water distilled
In autumn air, the gold of chrysanthemums.

In the jewelbox theater where I toiled
Two years or more in wonder and terror,
As soldier and wound-dresser, prisoner of war,
The footlights have gone out
With the damp-eyed ladies in velveteen
And men in waistcoats looped with golden chains,
Vowing to reduce war to pure science;
Gone into Manhattan's twilight and endless sleep.

The stage where the poet mourned his president
Is bare. Where shall we meet such heroes,
So justly grieved by grief so eloquent,
Or strong-limbed courage in a digital age?

Advertisement circa 1865

Young man, sober, strong, and trustworthy,
Stocked with a cork arm and leg of wood,
Will, for a decent salary and board,
Allow his fake limbs to be gnawed
By bears, wolves, or lions in any reputable
Menagerie. References on request. Will travel.

Photographer Unknown, Neuvilly, 1918

The light survives, exploding the north wall,
Splintering the vault above the side aisle,
Beaming upon the immobile white columns.
The church, surprised by so much radiance
Shelters the wounded soldiers, dark as pews,
Wound in army blankets, all equal now
In their suffering—blind, lame, or whole.
Who can tell the living from the dead,
Who suffered in brave silence or cried out
For medicine or mother? Not the doctors
Bending over the bodies, or armed captains
Judging who was ready to march again
Into the treacherous forest of Argonne.
Here the light has outlived the last man.

And what it saves is arbitrary, odd:
A spotted dog limping through rubble,
Some silver wickets of the altar rail,
A ladder angling from a chancel window,
So angels might visit if they pleased.
The altar is piled with guns and medicine,
And above it—as if art must have its say
Even now, in the ruins of a French town—
Hangs a life-sized canvas, a baroque scene
Of the Ascension. Christ hovers in the air
Above the stunned apostles, and His mother
In wide-eyed terror, calls to Him, "My son,
Remember me when Thy kingdom comes,
Leave me not long after Thee, my Son!"
For this was the seventh and final sorrow
Of the Virgin on earth, who then was left alone.

Iraq

I thought the war was wrong,
But stammered, tongue-tied
Between a howl and a song.
Not that the war was right
Or the men who made it just;
But to fight the good fight,
Each one in his way must
Guard what he knows best.

I know the human voice,
Gruff on the battleground,
Viaticum, the widow's cry.
Among these is no place
For political poetry,
Which being both is neither.
Too exacting of humankind
To forgive the lawmaker
Or soldier his assigned
Fault in the disaster.
Too pure and tenderhearted
To bear the weapons of peace
After the nightmare has started,
A poet is unfit for this,
Being more and less than human.
I shall try again and again
To countervail chaos,
Not as a poet, but as a man.

Democracy

On the way to City Hall he took a bribe,
Cash, too little to buy a good automobile,
Enough to pay one son's tuition bill.

When he got out of prison, the same tribe
Who'd courted him in power, and some others
Who'd loved him, couldn't look him in the eye.

Shame may turn wolves into lambs, force
Drunks to become saints, turn thorns by
And by into olives, but no treasury of remorse
Can purchase mercy from our cheated wards.

He wept and prayed, hoping his heart might break.
Spring came. And the lawmaker who had made
Young voters cheer and City Council quake,
Thrilled the ballpark, hawking lemonade.

The Battered Horn

Who has not done it, in the recklessness
Of youth, absentminded, or guiltily
At the end of night or debt-ridden day,
Taken someone else's words for ours,
Their thoughts or whiskey, wife or purse?

I have seen good newsmen given the ax
Because a line or two of common prose
Bolted the traces of quotation marks.
I don't mean to excuse the fake and robber.
Maybe they ought to hang every one of us

Who steal from nature and from one another.
And I say to the columnist under deadline:
If you covet a phrase or two of mine,
Take it—but beware the battered horn
Stolen from a thief long before you were born.

The Flood

Iam satis . . .
—HORACE

Palm trees shade the shores of Delaware;
Crocus and forsythia that signaled spring,
Bloom in winter, vexing the calendar.
What more do we need as an omen?
The last wedge of the icecap melting,
Or hurricanes to overturn a mountain?
People are frightened, recalling the Flood
When Noah built the ark, and a lost god
Drove seal herds over the Pyrenees;
Fish darted among the crowns of trees
Where owls and doves, suddenly homeless,
Once dwelled; deer swam until they drowned.

Maybe the Potomac will rise up
In tidal fury under a full moon, and
Batter the White House and the Capitol,
Flush every rat and serpent from his hole
Out to sea, so we might begin again.
Who among you would be shocked by this?
Our children, if any are left then,
Will curse us when they understand this war.
They shall hear how citizens drew their knives
And guns first upon one another,
Then shipped the young abroad to lose their lives.

Corrections

September 25, 2003

Yesterday's news of Kofi Annan's address
To the United Nations General Assembly
Garbled his complaint about the scarcity
Of rising nations on the Security Council.
He informed the delegates that unless
They address the issue with more care,
History won't "forgive us" (not "*forget* us").
The *Times* regrets the editing error.

An article about the Deputy Secretary
Of Defense's words at a forum on Iraq
Misstated the President's position about
Whether the cabinet of Saddam Hussein
Had contacts with Al Qaida, or not.
Mr. Bush said there was communication.
This is how rumors and wars get started;
The *Times* regrets mistaking fact for fiction.

Our column about the fire safety laws
Urged by those who studied the collapse
Of the Twin Towers, called a commissioner
Barbara who was Patricia—a transgression
We hope may be forgotten if not forgiven.
And the story of the woman fainting away
While skating, got the day of the Marathon
Wrong. It is run on Sunday, not Saturday.

The *Times* regrets all errors great and small,
Unjust reviews and character assassination.
We do our best to bring you the news daily
As we find it. While error is enormous

(To revise Bolingbroke ever-so-slightly),
Truth lies within a tiny and certain compass.
There's always tomorrow for us to get it right,
Unless the paper folds or the world ends.

5

Philosophers in a Meadow

Gaston Bachelard agrees
With wind-taming Empedocles:
In the soul's true meadow
No flower will grow
But the pale asphodel,
Which we know also
Flourishes in Hell.
And in the soul's meadow
The breath of wind
Failing to find
Melodious trees,
Must be content
To caress the silent
Waves of even grass.

Eurylochus Recalls the Sirens

When we returned from Hell, that sorceress
Who so loved our captain she set him free,
Feasted us with meat and bread and wine,
Praising us for our great-heartedness:
"In going down alive to the House of Hades,
You will have died twice instead of once—
Which is enough for any man to bear."
Sunset. And we sailors all lay down
To sleep by the stern cables of our ship.
But shapely Circe kept Odysseus up
Making love to him for the last time, again
And again, an infinity of kisses, and then
Warned him of the dangers that lay ahead.

Of Scylla and Charybdis I shall not speak,
For there are horrors memory consumes
With the men who are consumed by them.
Six comrades of my youth were plucked aloft
By that she-monster with six grinding mouths.
No mercy there, except their death was quick.

The Sirens cut the wound that would not heal.
Circe warned us of these cruel daughters
Of a sea-god, with the heads of lovely women,
And wings and feet of birds. They dwell
On an island near the whirlpool of Charybdis
Where they loll in a flowering meadow, waiting
For ships to pass. They know when to spring,
For Zeus has given them knowledge of everything.

Circe warned us not to sheer too close
To these harpies, or eavesdrop on their singing.
Wives and children will not welcome home

Men who've heard those voices clear and true.
Sirens perch on masts like cypress boughs
Of their island home where dead men's bones
Lie strewn, with flesh still clinging to them.
Circe bid us fill our ears with beeswax
To deafen us—all but Odysseus.
Why did she make exception for the man
She loved, why did she think he might
Listen harmlessly to what would kill us?
"Lash him to the crosspiece on the mast.
And when he begs and prays that you release him,
Tie him all the tighter the more he pleads."

The sorceress conjured up a favoring breeze
That swept us toward Sorrento and our fate.
Suddenly the bowl of the sea grew calm
As if it were a pond on a summer day,
And not a breath of wind to strum the water.
So we stowed the sails and set to rowing
While our captain carved a wheel of wax
Into wedges with his knife. In sunlight
He kneaded the wax and gently sealed our ears.
We tied him to the mast, and went on rowing.
Soon the Sirens mulled the air with music
Soft at first like a maiden's secret humming,
A serenade, or young mother's lullaby:
"Come, come, famous Odysseus, whose name
Brings eternal glory to the Achaeans,
Come listen to our ethereal harmonies.
No man with ears to hear can pass us by,
For wisdom sings the counterpoint to pleasure;
By Zeus, you shall know the past and future."

If the stars could sing in their heavenly courses;
If soft wind could intone the harp of branches;
If nightingales had accompanied Orpheus,
After the Sirens, they would seem like noise.
The maiden's chorale, the lady's serenade,
At last the rainbow of the coloratura
Pierced the melting beeswax of my ear:
So sad a beauty steeped in tragedy,
The melting minor strain of a threnody.
I heard little yet I heard too much.
Meanwhile Odysseus, the honored guest
Screamed at us, cursed, and chafed and writhed
As if he would tear free of his own skin,
Cried "Mutiny!" commanding we let him go.
I must say this was a vexing test,
As we were duty-bound to serve our captain.
But a voice inside us or above,
Made us true to more than the moment;
And so we tied him faster to the mast,
And bent our oars to escape the Sirens' sound.
So that curious danger, at least, was past.

Many a good man's death I have forgotten,
But not the Sirens' song. It seemed to pass
Into my heart although my ears were sealed.
I have no gift to set the melody
To words, but know the theme right well:
Of love lost, anguish, and the future gone.
Sometimes I hear the exquisite refrain,
Though kindly it grows fainter every day,
As if time and distance from that isle were one.

I welcome the hour that echo will die away.
As for our captain: Circe must have known
Her hero was not like the rest of us—
He could hear that tune with an open ear,
Banish it from his mind and not go mad.
Perhaps it was by grace of the Goddess
Athena, who dearly loved Odysseus,
And served him night and day as guardian.
As for me, I am a simple man
And welcome our voyage into the dark silence.

The White Quill

I sit on a rude bench under the maple tree
Watching sunrise open up the garden,
Dry the dew from the lawn, then turn
My dark windows above to glaring gold.
High overhead a squirrel is scurrying
Back and forth on a limb, with twigs
And leaves in his mouth, just frantic
To finish making his nest in the tree fork.
A few lyrate leaves rain down on me,
Stems corymbed with winged samara seeds.
My mind is on the character and fate
Of the man who toils behind one window,
Cloaked in darkness, then by dazzling light,
His crimes, lies and folly, work half done.

Here I am and there I am at once,
Spectacle and spectator, audience
And actor in a play without denouement,
Although I know how every knot was tied.
He sat under this tree before he died,
A squirrel above him scolding:
Get to work, you fool, winter is near.
Listen, man, there's no one behind the gold
Windowpane. That room is now for rent.
Look up and see what's drifting down to you,
Gliding and twirling on the autumn air:
A pale feather, longer than your hand,
White from pointed shaft to silken vane.
What kind of bird would drop from heaven
Such a pure quill, too large to be a dove's,
Too small and late for your great apology?

Old Man in Sun and Shadow

Of all my wordly goods and society,
Nothing is left but a table and chair,
A lamp casting dim light on a dark book,
And a grinning skull that will outstare
My blinking gaze unto eternity.

I gave my house to the homeless,
My money and shoes to the poor.
If that brings them no balm or happiness,
They are no worse off than before.
I gave my friends to each other,
My enemies to themselves. I pray
No favor of God or man except
Sunlight and silence where I might find
Some way to slow the minutes of a day,
Save motes of hours from Time's wind.

What have I given that I should have kept?
What have I kept I should have given away?

On a Theme of Ronsard

We die, then the rolling tide of years
Sweeps our works away all in due time.
God alone lasts. Of the human loom
Not a vein or sinew survives death,
Not a thought or feeling. The remnants
Are loose bones quartered in a lonely tomb.

Soul's joy is to behold God's radiance
And study its source; soul has no essence
But in this restless contemplation.
Happiness has little to do with this;
It comes from making family and verses,
A home, a garden, decent government,
None of which can gain a line or limb
From dust of those whom death has sent
Below. Therefore the bodiless realm
Of the hereafter has no police or laws,
No cities, jails, or theaters—no applause.

As for me: give me thirty years of fame
To revel in the light of the sun,
Good red wine and a woman for loving;
Let the Devil take the century of renown
After the sunken grave swallows my name.
Once a man has passed beyond the days
When he can be moved and not just moving,
What is left has no more need of praise.

Heading Home

I watched the miles, I saw my life go by,
A drumbeat of bare trees and frozen ponds,
Forlorn stations, ruined factories.
I must have dozed, my head against the glass.
Women I dreamed I would have died for once
Mourned me in a dream. South by southwest
Our train cleaved the horizon, pushed the sun
Toward somebody else's sunrise, while
Heaven and earth denied my day was done,
Painting a fantastic continent
Of cumulus and ether, air and mist,
Real as any land to a waking man.
A wall of purple hills sloped to the shore
In fluted cliffs; cloud archipelagos
Edged with golden beaches jeweled a sea
Bluer than our sky. Had I missed my stop?
Now was I on my way out of this world,
Alone on the express to Elysium,
Lotus trees, the lost woman of my dreams?

Shadows deepened and the speeding train
Rolled on into twilight. Slowly then
I came to myself, cold, woke to the thought:
This is how it must be at the end of the line.
You cannot tell the water from the sky,
Mourners from the dead, or clouds from land.
The fire of the sun has tricked you blind,
And earth, air and water join in one.

Codicil

Vain men postpone their wills
Despite all rhyme and reason
In the toll of the church bells,
Thinking to outwit fate—
Because no sensible person
Would trust his gifts to the state.

But this happens every day
As the superstitious scheme
To hold Death at bay
Delays the signature
Meant to rescue and redeem
Control over the future.

My children, I write to you,
Being of sound mind,
As far as a man can know.
I am not rich or poor;
I am neither cruel nor kind
But your thinking makes it so.

I gave you life and give it again
Each dawn, the earth, and stars,
The wind, the sun, and rain,
The choice between good and evil.
I gave you sisters and brothers
To love. Think of me as you will.